D0792448

for Ishaan

This is about saving the cat...

or not.

ACKNOWLEDGMENTS

I'm grateful to Susan Gardner for her enduring commitment to bringing beauty to the world. Her vision, dedication, and creativity shine through all she touches. Thank you, Susan, for all you've done to make this a better book.

A special thank you to April Ossmann for her wonderful insights that clarified and strengthened the poems.

Thank you, also, to Jennifer Givhan for her honest appraisals and enlivening suggestions.

Thank you, Alberto Ríos, for your continued support and generosity of spirit. You are amazing!

I am grateful to California State University, Fullerton, for a sabbatical during which this collection truly came into its own.

For Ellen Caldwell—friend extraordinaire, teacher, scholar, and all around amazing human being. So much sings in the world because of you.

I thank my family, again and again, for the love and support; my students, who have taught me so much; my poetry partners, Jie Tian and Natalie Graham, who keep the words alive; my colleagues who have challenged and strengthened me; and, most of all, Ishaan—always an inspiration.

Nanquan Kills a Cat

Introduction: Kick over the ocean and dust flies on the earth; scatter the clouds with shouts, and empty space shatters. Strictly executing the true imperative is still half the issue; as for the complete manifestation of the great function, how do you carry it out?

Case: One day at Nanquan's the eastern and western halls were arguing over a cat. When Nanquan saw this, he took it and held it up and said, "If you speak I won't cut it."
The group had no reply; Nanquan then cut the cat in two.
Nanquan also brought up the foregoing incident to Zhaozhou and asked him: Zhaozhou immediately took off his sandals, put them on his head, and left.
Nanquan said, "If you had been here you could have saved the cat."

—*The Book of Serenity*, tr. Thomas Cleary

I

Since his deployment, morning shadows haunt the toaster, microwave, knife block—so she heads out for coffee. The disposable cup swallowed behind a swinging trash bin door echoes throughout her day, a click in her jaw that never really goes away.

Spare the rod and spoil the child.

—Samuel Butler

THIS WILL GROW HAIR ON YOUR CHEST

Steel cylinders
of milk, cream, non-fat
milk, and half-
and-half scrum
on doctoring stations
littered with torn
packets, spent sugar,
and broken stirring sticks.
Shoulders clinking
like bargained coins,
rigid as soldiers
in their plastic-
capped chrome,
snipers who deliver
their shots to soften
coffee meant
to stiffen
our selves.

Palate drying, he drops the second handful of kale back in the bag, places the smaller saucepan on the stove. Should he cook all the chicken, or only the piece he'll eat tonight? No placemat. The only thing he'll look at is the plate.

A hypsochromic shift marks the change of a spectral band to a shorter wavelength and higher frequency. As the color blue has a shorter wavelength, a hypsochromic shift is also referred to as a "blue shift."

If I don't have red, I use blue.

—Pablo Picasso

HYPSOCHROMIC SHIFT

Maple, plastic, even glass parries
the knife edge without spalling,
shielding the counter beneath.

Quick as thought, the blade
cleaving pork, apples, onions,
beets, changes clip

from measured even slicing
steady as a resting pulse
to castaneting,

high-beat chopping.
Stoic, but not impervious,
violence scars its face,

yet the board stays whole
enough to hold parings, bones,
and marrow, absorbing force,

deconstructing what we eat
until each bite's easier to swallow.

Years back, they struggled through the conversations about belief, their differences settled. Making eye contact in the mirror, they brush teeth side by side. He sees that all she sees is what's acceptable, the rest of him flaked off, a lesser, thinner, version of him not him at all. She sees he cannot see, slow worm, she's cheating on him.

One of the four fundamental forces of nature (the others are gravity, electromagnetic force, and weak force), strong nuclear force holds subatomic particles in the nucleus together. It also binds quarks into protons and neutrons. The strong force has a very short range.

Life is an illusion. I am held together in the nothingness by art.

— Anselm Kiefer

STRONG NUCLEAR FORCE

It's not always pretty, what holds us together.
In foyers, kitchens, bathrooms, eyes rest
on mosaicked peacocks, mother-of-pearl
lilies, orange blossoms, daffodils
overlooking the interstitial grout keeping
their marriages sound. Scrubbed with the thinnest

of stiff-bristle brushes, even when mold
and mildew discolor it and can't be flaked
away from the tear-resistant lines,
the grit-graced cement of stubbornness
defies gravity and balances the tesserae,
bound to their pattern, defying decay.

Salvation is a solitary path. She accepts the loss of friends along the way. Never pushy, she gently reminded them when eating out about the wisest food choices, how many calories in the breakfast platter and how much sodium, of course. She said these things out of love. And she still loves them. All of them. Wishing them well, even if no one eats with her anymore.

The Nevi'im Acharonim are the latter prophets of the Hebrew Bible. Major Nevi'im Acharonim are Isaiah, Jeremiah, and Ezekiel.

One must be a sea, to receive a polluted stream without becoming impure.

—Friedrich Nietzsche

NEVI'IM ACHARONIM

The furnace exhales
heat from the ceiling,
floor, and wall—metal
slats parsing climates.

To exist, expel.
Change the local
atmosphere. Vent
prophetic tales
of mold, of dust,
abandoned webs
and shriveled pests

drawn from the inner
ducts—a building's
breath let loose,
withering the plants
that would die of cold
if returned to the open air.

He couldn't figure where the pressure came from. In line at the DMV, again, waiting to pay a ticket, a blister against his heel from boots he'd worn pain free for years. Why now? What changed?

It may not be nice to be good, little 6655321. It may be horrible to be good. And when I say that to you I realize how self-contradictory that sounds. I know I shall have many sleepless nights about this. What does God want? Does God want goodness or the choice of goodness? Is a man who chooses the bad perhaps in some way better than a man who has the good imposed upon him? Deep and hard questions, little 6655321.

—Anthony Burgess, *A Clockwork Orange*

WAR ON POVERTY

Drains throat more than water—
spiraling soap, hair, dirt, grease,
cleanser, champagne
grapes, spit, toothpaste,
a river of waste we launch
earthward. We know well enough,
standing in the tub's refusing-
to-empty slick, lowering hands
in oily gray dishwater to finger
out clogs—no matter how we malign
the suck of energy, we need
a drain's down so we can clean up.

He locked the doors. He had to. He needed to be alone when he felt this good. No one could keep up with him. The relief. The rush, soaking in it, air in his lungs forever. Until it waned. He wanted no one leaning over him after he hit the floor.

Porifera is the name of a phylum that encompasses more than 5,000 species of sponges. The fossil record offers evidence for the existence of sponges in the Cryogenian period 635 to 720 million years ago.

Book III of Vitruvius's ten-volume *De Architectura* provided inspiration for Leonardo da Vinci's Vitruvian Man drawing.

Marble is not alike in all countries.

—Vitruvius

PORIFERA

Sprouting
even from your broken
bits, no brain, no heart,
no stomach,
lacking symmetry,
an absorbing earth
welcoming seeds,
your pocked, porous
architecture
teases crumbs
from the sad
perpetuity of tides.

Soft, permeable,
you hold water,

but not like a glass
or bucket
with their stuck-at-O
rigidity.

What if you had served
as blueprint,
dabbing wounds,
soothing fevers,
wetting lips
at the end?

The paper wrinkled under her as she tried to pull the gown closed in front, the tie-strings shriveled from over washing. They'd open it to check the breasts later. The room's offensively inoffensive greens, and taupes, and blues, grayed toward institutional. This minute before the doctor belonged to her: awkward, cold. In ten minutes, they'd wipe what was left of her off the bench and spread paper for the next one.

A 2014 *Financial Times* article by James Kynge, "Emerging Markets: Fear of Contagion," focused on emerging economies (Argentina, Brazil, Russia, Turkey, Indonesia) and what is identified as the "contagious" weakness of their currencies against the US dollar.

Ancient Egyptian tombs included paintings of doors, passageways to the afterlife. The Roman architect Vitruvius suggested stiles and rails as frames for doors.

Light's journey across the floor over the course of a day imitates the minute- and hour-hands' journey around the clock face, absent from digital displays.

There is no blue without yellow and without orange.

—Vincent van Gogh

"Emerging Markets: Fear of Contagion"

In the beginning was
no door, just a way
in or out. Day's light angles
along the ground
sweeping the hours,
night sky inside,
sunflower outside,
a kinship
in commerce, one.

When preventing ingress
or egress with skin
or cloth proved inadequate,
bronze-bound wood and, of course,
the hinge filled in.
With a hinge
comes a handle, with a handle,
a lock. But outsiders
who rattled a knob
left marauders: germs.

Better to go automatic,
with no one touching
doors you can always choose
to keep locked.

Out the window, she sees the shantytown other students hobbled together to protest for divestment. She envies their lack of concern for making a scene. They don't care about causing trouble, being thrown out. She can't afford mistakes. Her parents sacrificed and limped on, broken, for her to be here—though the longer she stays the further away her parents get. They love her, they want the best for her, and every visit home they understand her less. She pulls on her backpack, heavy with anthologies. She'll walk silently through the protestors on her way to class.

Setting a pick in sports applies here—(I sit in the back row looking down at the book, eyes stinging, other students turned toward me in confusion or protest—*the author's a child of immigrants…he loves these people.* The teacher smiles good-humoredly: *You're reading it wrong.* I have no words. Someone described, no, someone describes my parents as animals, and I have no words).

Gallup finds education to be the greatest difference between the wealthiest 1% of Americans and everyone else. The Gallup analysis reveals that 72% of the wealthiest Americans have a college degree, compared with 31% of those in the lower 99 percentiles. Furthermore, nearly half of those in the wealthiest group have postgraduate education, versus 16% of all others.

—*The Gallup Poll: Public Opinion 2011*, ed. Frank Newport

American Dream

I have lived
in homes without them,
built in the days

of flyswatters
grown uncommon
through our love

of screens designed
to keep insects out,
not vision in—

Not the wood and silk
of three-fold frames
to dress behind,

not the smoke
hiding attack
or retreat,

not the flat, vast
space where shadow-
light plays

make us feel
we see life
till the wall

re-blanks
then what
a tremendous

waste of space
the movie's empty
canvas becomes.

Quite plain, really,
sight undisturbed
by irritants,

thin, networked wires,
invisible from a distance,
today a gray haze

before windows
and doors,
with weaves so small

no would-be explorer
bird, bee,
or wasp, can enter,

but strong and fine
enough for those inside
to see them try.

The first bump stock was the hardest to buy, not because it was tricky to get my hands on, but because of how it felt inside, given my plans. What if the seller knew? What if I looked too nervous, too twitchy, too cold? But nobody cared. Nobody asked, "What do you want this for?" as if the answer were already plain.

Mark this well, you proud men of action! You are, after all, nothing but unconscious instruments of the men of thought.

—Georg Wilhelm Friedrich Hegel

CALLING THE SHOTS

Eight ball
corner pocket.
Tequila.
Vodka.
Jello.
Lung. Heart.
Right foot.
Left temple:
Don't move
until I tell
you.

Their eyes pick you out and wall you off without their needing to say a thing. You'd think just walking down a street, going where you need to go, wouldn't register with others—and for some it doesn't. But there are those to whom your simply being there is a bother. They make you feel it. More than a passing glance, a kind of looking up and down, something angry, something dismissive, something that says, "You don't belong."

After similar protests by Claudette Colvin, Aurelia S. Browder, Susie McDonald, and Mary Louise Smith, Rosa Parks was arrested for refusing to relinquish her bus seat to a white male passenger. The Montgomery Bus Boycott that followed led to the November 13, 1956 Browder v. Gayle US Supreme Court decision, which struck down Alabama state and Montgomery city public transportation segregation laws.

And even though I have to face the prospect of being a minority of one, I humbly believe I have the courage to be in such a hopeless minority.

—Mahatma Gandhi

Montgomery, Alabama, December 1, 1955

Remaining steadfast—
a barycenter, a hinge
uniting chapters
of the story—requires
iron discipline.

One wing nailed
to the door,
the other
to the jamb,
pinched when closed.
The spine straight,

the body's sections spin
around the central
spike. Without
these pinned, brass plates,

palms that meet
in thought or prayer—
the closed door
will not open
for your quest.

Using intarsia as her mother taught her, she chooses the brightest yellows, reds, and blues. The only sound inside her house is needles rhythmically clicking as she works the yarn knitting booties for the grandson she hasn't met. He's three months old already, on the other side of the continent, a child who has her eyes, she's told, without her ever laying eyes on him.

Derived from the highly poisonous sap of *Toxicodendron vernicifluum*, lacquer contains urushiol (also found in poison ivy). Even the vapor can cause rashes.

The quote below is taken from: "Propositions made by His Excellency William Burnet…to the five Nations to wit the Mohogs, Oneydes Onondages, Cayauges & Sinnekees in Albany 27 day of August 1722."

Brethren
Our last meeting ended with so happy an Agreement & such firm assurances and hearty resolutions on both sides, that if they are faithfully observ[d] we shall always meet with joyful countenances.

—William Burnet

INTARSIA

Because feet freeze
and rocks scrape toes,

because passages
beckon and children

slide on lacquered floors,
because the body

sprouts nails,
callouses over, grows

fevered, old, and slow—
because love,

      loop click,
       after *loop click*

strives to keep up with it.

The food looks different, no fruits or vegetables to bite into, just cubes, without skin, cooked soft. The plate's divided. One type of food never touches another. All the liquids come in boxes. He remembers watching hands stir, and shape, and serve his food. He can't imagine the hands that prepared what's on his tray. He doesn't know where anyone he loves is. He'll only eat because he's hungry.

Adsorption, the binding of particles to a surface, differs from absorption in which particles fill holes in a solid.

[I]t is a happy faculty of the mind to slough that which conscience refuses to assimilate.

—William Faulkner

ADSORPTION

Placed at the foot,
a "WELCOME"
for eyes cast down,
the doormat
invites guests to slough
the dust of travels,
averting damage
to cream carpets, tiles,
and entryways.

Belittled for its conciliatory posture,
bowing below the stiles
of interpersonal commerce,
this tough, bristled back
of the sacred
accepts the dirt
we never believe
we carry with us.

She's infuriating! As if I don't know what I like. She's always insisting, always pushing: *this sweater matches your eyes, that skirt's too short, those shoes will turn your ankle.* Why doesn't she micromanage her own mess of a life?

A Gravity Tractor is a theoretical aircraft that would gradually nudge a space object, such as an asteroid, out of earth's orbit, preventing impact.

The thing that is important is the thing that is not seen.

—Antoine de Saint-Exupéry, *The Little Prince*

GRAVITY TRACTOR

How many times
have I borne

your paranoia?
Phantom smoke

escaping the broiler
or bacon frying

in the pan
inspires that mother's

shriek at her child
who never dreamed

of touching the skillet
ten feet away.

To a detector,
all the credulous play

with fire. Vigilant
to a fault, primed for one

response, you screech
at hints of danger.

Only if you someday save me
will I understand your love.

My office has the best view, better even, than grandfather's. They'd be envious if they knew. At night, lights stream away in rivers, white approaching, red retreating. I stay here later and later just to look at it. My window, a rectangle of light at the top of a dark tower—I bet they eat their hearts out when they see it.

There are painters who transform the sun into a yellow spot, but there are others who with the help of their art and their intelligence transform a yellow spot into the sun.

—Pablo Picasso

CLOTHES MAKE THE MAN

Hooked in a row,
my robes and sweaters
stretch long and thin
as muskellunge, or northern pike.

I'd rather hook than hang,
catch and release
my clothes without
the idle chatter
of sliding hangers.

On wounded days,
I don't want a human
shape, that headless
neck and shoulder
mimicry haunting
my unworn clothes.

Forty years she'd been teaching, 40 years of correcting pronunciations of Chaucerian English, of supporting interpretations, of signing off on, then typing up, then digitally submitting grad checks for students, thousands of them commencing toward their lives. This is what there was, the whole world, a single thread spiraling from an office.

I like a view, but I like to sit with my back turned to it.

—Gertrude Stein, *The Autobiography of Alice B. Toklas*

AUTOBIOGRAPHY

Steeled by hunger
for the art,
the nail behind
the painting,
supports in hiding
like a lynchpin operative,
or an angel
in the house.
Would you drop
what you love
to be seen
as you are?
A sixth blind man
still unaware
of the stumble
that will topple him
out-glories
one slim brainstem
to this Brueghel,
but the art's
elevation hangs
by a primal thread,
a glint we believe in
yet cannot see,
like our sidereal ancestry.
The painting keeps
its back to the nail
holding its love.
Not being seen
as it is,
makes it
all it is.

If you move far and fast enough, you never need to open up the coffin of your heart. Travel light. Free. Pick up pleasure, then move on. Fed for now. Don't worry about higher, about deeper. Go over, go around, not into. Everything's a breeze. Easy. Comfortable. Don't follow those trapped suckers who want, who need, who yearn. Most end up bitter. Most don't know: The purity of joy will rip you apart.

Given their thin muscular skin and the demands of movement within water, jellyfish shouldn't be able to grow beyond three centimeters in diameter. But large jellyfish species measuring more than two meters in diameter do exist; a special propulsion method allows them to move without splitting.

12a þæt biþ in eorle	that it is in men
indryhten þeaw,	a noble custom,
þæt he his ferðlocan	that one should keep secure
fæste binde,	his spirit-chest,
ealed his hordcofan,	guard his treasure-chamber,
hycge swa he wille.	think as he wishes.

—Anonymous, *The Wanderer*

The Jellyfish Paradox

Designed
like the most naïve heart
to be opened, filled,
and emptied again,
wallet, pens,
tissues, books,
stretch the purse
to bursting—
yet the seams don't give
(o soul that won't

let go, mind
that won't forget).
Overturned
on the floor,
no amount
of repacking
makes it lighter
or leads
us to forgetfulness,
that inner country
far away from home.

II

I open all the windows for the pre-morning drive across the desert, even in winter when my breath steams out of me. It's quiet, the low scrub becoming visible against the sandy backdrop as I head home from work. All night, I've been hitting targets on the other side of the world—for real, though it looks like a game. Even with the windows open, I can't escape the pointed accusations of that ball of fire mounting the horizon.

If your hate could be turned into electricity, it would light up the whole world.

—Nikola Tesla

US PATENT 613,809: REMOTE CONTROL

What an achievement!
An empire
in your hand—
power to kill
the show that drones
on, or target faces
flickering over
the screen.
Not because you can't
go, but because you don't
want to. Relax. Sit back.
Decide how long
the lights will play
before you snuff
them out.

They laughed when I said things no one should say in polite company. They cheered me on. It was easy, swelling the underbelly of bias, of prejudice. They roared my name, jumped from their seats applauding. It's not that I hated anybody, or even believed what I said. I liked being wanted, hungered for; I liked people clamoring, shouting, lining up to see someone who wasn't me.

Discussions and scholarly disagreements continue regarding the reasons why the Norse abandoned their Greenland settlements in the 15ᵗʰ century.

The values to which people cling most stubbornly under inappropriate conditions are those values that were previously the source of their greatest triumphs over adversity.

—Jared Diamond, *Collapse: How Societies Choose to Fail or Succeed*

Greenland Norse

Avoid the fault lines and wrinkles in the crust
where one tectonic sheet tugs another to its chin.
Reconsider flood plains. Remember,
seaside hills with ocean views dissolve to mud
in record-setting rainfall years. Who controls
the twisting claws of fire or soothes
the cranky temperaments of craters shrugging
off their ice-age naps? Seek out bedrock—
seamless, lasting, stable. Build there.
Forget the back-road drives past ruins
with their uncracked bases, roofs and walls
collapsed, their chimneys' forlorn steeples
pointing toward an empty up
when even firm foundations weren't solid enough.

I was somebody, right, because I was there, watching that blast light the desert, thrilled by what we'd done—and terrified. For really, I was no one, not a name to recall. Surrounded by others, each with a hand in what we'd made, all celebrating, I shrank to one speck in my mind's expanding universe, smaller and smaller, and still less now, as space stretches out in all directions, with no chance, none at all, to even matter as matter.

In 1998, Pakistan tested weapons under the Koh Kambaran (Ras Koh Hills).

Known as the eternal file of Bab Gurgur, a large oil field near Kirkuk in northern Iraq has been burning for 2,500 years.

How nice—to feel nothing, and still get full credit for being alive.

—Kurt Vonnegut, *Slaughterhouse Five*

Koh Kambaran, 1998

The pilot light
glows in the well
before explosions—
we high-medium-low
the burner's
blue crown, torque
the oven's furnace,
from bake to cremate.
The flame floats,
constant as Baba Gurgur's,
steady as peace,
till we force controlled
eruptions in the name
of survival,
frying, roasting, boiling.
Lose that light,
and destruction breeds,
the smallest spark
birthing annihilation
from visibly
immaculate air.

He remembers less and less of me, although I visit every day. First, it was my name. Then, he'd have to be reminded I'm his son. A few times he thought I was my brother, who doesn't visit, but whom he recalls in more detail. One day, I became a nice person visiting. Then, a stranger every time I walked into the room.

Give me the waters of Lethe that numb the heart, if they exist, I will still not have the power to forget you.

—Ovid

Alzheimer's Disciples

I.

We begin
with connection,
viviparous,
anchored in amniotic seas,
developing in the soft-
shelled egg of the womb.
We live with the scar
of removal,
our umbilicals
mimicked in a world
of buried wires,
cables plugged
into the wall's navel,
powering our lights
and laptops.

II.

When party lines
meant more than political affiliations
or queues outside raves,
and neighbors listened in
without surveillance systems,
we perched on kitchen chairs,
beneath the wall mount,
those short, spiraled cords
the bane of teen existence,
one jack for a family
of six, every sibling knowing
who called for whom.

III.

Pulled off at the root,
cordless, wireless,
satellites shoot
star-like through space
at 17,000 miles per hour,
to keep us virtually
connected.

IV.

No need to remember,
never lost, a battery
of signals monotoning
directions—prepare
to merge, turn
right, arrive at destination—

or pass, distracted,
turn left, turn
left, turn left,
circling the gravity
of a lost center,

failing to follow
the thread
of four stray notes
from childhood,
baa, baa, black sheep…

baa, baa, black sheep…
bye-bye, bye-bye.

The harder you work, the better you are, right? I arrive when the sun roses the walls of the buildings and stay until lights star the darkness. Sometimes I have to keep the door open, but I don't like to because I get less done—people want to chat about the game or what they did on Saturday. I come to work, but they don't want to hear that. It's quiet here, nights and weekends, holidays, too—hours and hours uninterrupted.

But she straighter walked for Freight

—Emily Dickinson, "Had we known the Ton she bore"

RADIUM ($_{88}$RA)

Set in the burner's
well, an iron
trivet primed

by the burden
of the seam,
you survived

the blast furnace.
Cast to endure
scalding and scrubbing,

overshadowed
by what you helped create—
no vat of boiling

water ever tipped
on your watch—
you give while holding

strong, holding
on, holding up
and never crumbling.

Hey! You made it out tonight! I love this bar, don't you? Look there's Joe. I'm going to say Hi. How about another beer? You're not going to drink slow tonight, are you? Oh my God how great to see you. Let me hug you, man! Who's that? Whoa! It's been like years since I saw you. What's happening? Hey did you see that one who just walked in? Whaddaya think of that, eh? Pretty good? Or that one over there? Look who it is! You don't go out so often, do you? Me? I just got here, but I plan to stay.

Some animals possess aposematism, a particular color or marking that warns predators of toxic traits such as poisonous venom or stingers.

There is one who remembers the way to your door: Life you may evade, but Death you shall not.

—T.S. Eliot, "Choruses from 'The Rock'"

APOSEMATISM

The cabinet mirror
convexes my blemished
skin, my sleep-stained face.
I don't remember looking
this bad,
but the magnet yields
with a reassuring click—
What a relief!
My reflection's replaced
by shelves
of treatments.
Mint-green toothpaste's
quick-brush cure
for mossy morning teeth.
Pink for upset stomach,
a full spectrum
of headache options,
cures for rashes,
dried-out contacts,
coughs and fevers,
cuts and scrapes—
who'd think so much
could go wrong and does?
I've yet to mention
all the push-down-
while-turning capped
brown vials, after which
I close the cabinet.
No need to look closer—
I could kill me.

The world's loud—rushing, insisting, shifting. I move through the dark of 3 a.m. for the quiet, knowing that someone else is awake, and feels the night, and lets it be. Long before dawn provokes them, cars wake up.

Diel vertical migration involves the upward movement of numerous species of plankton and other animals from one zone of an ocean or lake to the surface. Rather than being prompted by the sun, the migration usually occurs at night and the animals feed in the surface waters before descending. It is the largest migration, in terms of biomass, on the planet.

The mesopelagic, also known as the twilight zone, extends from 200 to 1,000 meters below the surface.

Starling murmurations rely on scale-free correlation, a critical system tipping point phenomenon also at work in particle physics and avalanches, with each bird coordinating individual and group movement with the six or seven birds closest to it.

A physicist is just an atom's way of looking at itself.

—Niels Bohr

Diel Vertical Migration

We stagger shingles,
          magazine-racking
tar-backed leaflets
          only birds
or gods will read,
          our peaked roofs
angling against
          what the heavens drop.
Housed under
          slate layers
or wooden shakes
          floated skyward
like mesopelagic
          migrants, we forget
the misery
          of drenching
and the history
          of burnt poems rising,
like scatter-wing starlings,
          to the top of it all.

Thinking about an individual, you lose the big picture. Ideals require sacrifice. They are troops for a reason, not a list of names, not mouths to feed, just battalions receiving rations. This is not the time for personal stories, but for larger victories. I am the name that decides it all.

Georgy Zhukov was the Russian general who captured Berlin during WWII. He had a reputation for accepting heavy losses and later in his career, oversaw a disastrous Russian nuclear weapons test. An environmental catastrophe, it possibly killed thousands, though numbers were not disclosed.

All violence consists in some people forcing others, under threat of suffering or death, to do what they do not want to do.

—Leo Tolstoy, *A Confession and Other Religious Writings*

Zhukov Lights the Samovar for Afternoon Tea

They lie, row flat on row, tip
to tip, imprisoned in boxes
stacked on shelves. They survived
the lightning strike to be fragged
by the saw. Cut off from histories
of sun, or wind, or ocean storms,
not chosen for a book, but a box,
they'd swap stories with the cardboard
if they could. Perhaps they fear

unnatural selection, being dragged
across the filing until friction
gutters their fire free—lightning's
shock having caught them anyway.
Is the safety of the box
preferable to burning?

Cast in plays of light—
clandestine meetings with a wick,
martyrdom in fireplace hell,
the hopeless romance of kissing
a cigarette tip—they burn
with a flame insisting upward
only to be charred, spent, dropped,
and abandoned to earth.

A limb, immobile, useless, lonely for its body, never dreams, that an imposter — clumsy, cold, stiff with certainty and promises of reliability — has already replaced it.

Operation Menu, former President Nixon's covert bombing campaign, dropped 108,823 tons of ordnance on Cambodia from March 1969 to May 1970. The first run was called Breakfast. Later missions were named Lunch, Snack, Dinner, Supper, and Dessert.

Q: Most land mines, bombs, or cluster bombs are reportedly made by Russia, China and America. Are there any calls to hold these countries to account for 40,000 Cambodian amputees and the thousands who were killed by the weapons they produced?

A: Our effort here is not to find out who is to blame. When there is a war, everybody gets impacted, and everybody gets impacted in many, many different ways—some people more than others.... What we're really focusing on is helping the government of Cambodia find these mines, dig them up, and make their country safe for the generation of people who are still in Cambodia today and then hopefully for the future—for the children that are out there.

—Sarada Taing interview with Rear Admiral Samuel Perez Jr., "Clearing Cambodia of Landmines by 2015 was Unrealistic," Radio Free Asia, February 27, 2015.

OPERATION MENU

Scrubbing to make clean,
something else gets dirty.
In the theater of maintaining
appearances, the soap dish grays
with scum, worse than the sink.

Washing hands before meals
with French-milled, Lava,
Caress, each molded
rose or shell worn to a nub
of godliness-evoking cleanliness,

sloughs off grit.
Sluicing slicks the dish,
till the impoverished soap
skitters across the tub,
pocked by the yawning drain.

An offered palm or crater,
our self-claimed landfill's parallel scars,
plastered with muck,
raise the soap to dry out,
clean as our living.

"The imp of the perverse" flashes images in your mind at the most inopportune times—horrifying, intriguing. Who knew the neighbor's dog could make you think that? How did this get inside? How can it live there when you do everything you can to shut it down, deny, and silence it? Good thing no one else can see the rot within you. Keep fighting. Keep those thoughts down. You have no idea how it keeps you alive.

Samarium, a rare earth metal (REM), is highly magnetic and is utilized in headphones and carbon arc lighting as well as in precision guided munitions. Essential to a wide range of technological applications, rare earth metals (REMs) are not necessarily rare but are highly dispersed in the Earth's crust, often found together, they are difficult to separate and extract in large amounts.

I am a forest, and a night of dark trees: but he who is not afraid of my darkness, will find banks full of roses under my cypresses.

—Friedrich Nietzsche, *Thus Spake Zarathustra*

SAMARIUM (₆₂SM)

How duplicitous the knife,
tempered as it is,
for I've pressed my fingers,
even my tongue, along the flat
licking the last smear of goat
cheese and look! No harm.

See this sliver gut tomatoes,
scallop muscles beneath ashy-eyed
potato skin, and tear flesh
from the peach pit's dark wood wrinkles.

How many edges pare the blemish—
for what exists without one—
or trim the food, bit by bit,

for a child's small mouth?

Carving finer than fingers
or teeth alone, weapon, tool,
sheathed in the heart of my kitchen—
I sense violence
in convenience.

See the difference:
It steals the breath
when the knife is raised
companion to the fist.

I don't mind the early hours. When else do I see empty freeway lanes, as if all of them were made for me, just take my pick and get there fast? I'm not the one who takes your money. I'm not the one who cooks your food. I mop the floors, see to the bathroom, ensure you have a pleasant visit. You'll only see me if I fail.

Yttrium, often classified as a rare earth metal, is used in the creation of LEDS, lasers, superconductors, and microwave filters. It strengthens magnesium and aluminum alloys.

In 2013, the 3.3 million workers whose wages were at or below the federal minimum made up 4.3 percent of all hourly paid workers.

—U.S. Bureau of Labor Statistics

YTTRIUM ($_{39}$Y)

The rack suffers like a prophet—
Jonah in the mouth
of the oven, holding
dinner on his back—
a disciplined emissary
of four hundred-degree situations.

Exposure to heat
is not exposure
to fire: one bakes,
the other burns
the bread.

The rack responds to commands,
closer to flames or farther away,
chosen to endure hell
as long as required to keep us fed.

Blending in provides your shell: Wear this year's styles, nothing fancy; drive a gray, beige, or light blue car. Thank God it's easy to find top-ten music and TV shows. Don't think too much about what happens next or people ask questions. Never let the questions begin. How would you hide? Nod just enough. Smile, but not enthusiastically. Tap in time with the music. Let someone else set the course. Don't worry. Follow. Most people want to arrive and won't lead you off a cliff.

Carcinology is the study of crustaceans.

I seem to have been only like a boy playing on the seashore, and diverting myself in now and then finding a smoother pebble or a prettier shell than ordinary, whilst the great ocean of truth lay all undiscovered before me.

—Isaac Newton

CARCINOLOGY

The dragged refrigerator,
punched saucer signatures
of plastic casters
shoeing table legs,
a child's footprint
of how-to-pound-
blocks knowledge—
scarred the linoleum.
Designed in a time
when mushroom clouds
vaporized the last angels,
builders hermit-crabbed kitchens
into that season's mass-produced
right angles, an expanding universe
of streaks and globs of gray
and taupe on off-white or black,
the scattering fragments
of some great blast
a perfect exoskeleton.
Heel and boot marks,
a chemical spill that left
an inky stain, the cracks of age,
so what if the dropped knife
claws the surface, the milk spills,
or the newly laid carpet sands
beige dust over everything?
Our dark-sky shell
of no-wax chaos
shields us from everyday
betrayals easily enough.

The cushion, grayed with oils, holds the imprint of a body no longer here. A favorite spot, windows to the right, TV screen ahead, a little light when nothing's on in early afternoon. The chair embraced more, but the footrest held the earthbound, the callused soles, knowing they were always on their way somewhere else.

Neodymium is a rare earth metal. Never found as a free element, it is separated from ores (usually monazite and bastnäsite) and used in the creation of lasers, light bulbs, tinting glass, and lighter flints. Its exceptionally strong magnetic qualities are used in computers, cell phones, and medical equipment.

It is from metaphor that we can best get hold of something fresh. When the poet calls "old age a withered stalk," he conveys a new idea, a new fact, to us by means of the general notion of bloom, which is common to both things.

—Aristotle, *Rhetoric*

NEODYMIUM (60ND)

Lacking thrones' glamour,
but vehicles of elevation
nonetheless, footstools
raise the heels that know
the ground best.

Head, torso, arms, almost forget
gravity's demands, floating
as they do. Feet, manacled
to the love of the core
of the spinning Earth,
release above-the-knee selves
toward flight. So why not
free the soles a short

leap above a world
that won't otherwise let them go?

Whenever I see them inside, I spray. I only use the paper towels for wiping up after. I don't see the point of crunching a roach or ant when poison's handy, though the smell tends to linger.

Operation Ranch Hand was the name of a US military operation that sprayed Agent Orange and other herbicides in Southeast Asia during the Vietnam War.

As long as this policy stands, no operation like Ranch Hand could happen again.

—William Buckingham, Jr., *Operation Ranch Hand: The Air Force and Herbicides in Southeast Asia, 1961-1971*

Our Goose Is Cooked

Before engineered ovens,
we shifted firewood and pans,
risking burned fingers to prevent
scorching the lamb.
Now, numbered dials dictate temps
and thermostats tick off

the rising heat. Settling
by degrees on three
hundred fifty, relaxing—then blasting

hot air, obeying a higher directive,
the bursts of fire, express
and repeat, express and repeat
(while we vase flowers, toss
salad), until our dinner's done.

I sleep during the day now. At night, I walk the halls, darkness or moonlight priming the walls, and I see them wandering, looking into rooms, wordlessly passing each other. They're younger than I am, seemingly on their way somewhere, but going nowhere. My whole life they've been looking for me. Now that they're near, they don't care that I'm here.

Consort of Chronos, Ananke is the mother of the fates and is sometimes depicted holding a spindle.

We construct a narrative for ourselves, and that's the thread that we follow from one day to the next. People who disintegrate as personalities are the ones who lose that thread.

—Paul Auster

ANANKE

I see the ghost of a hinge
   in you, spool—spine straight,
     top and bottom flanges jutting
   like the covers of a book—
not the narrative itself, but a bone
   holding the flesh of a story
     spun to plumpness,
   then thinning along
each labyrinth as you're used—
   quickly for a new dress,
     slowly for mending. Turn one way
   to accept, the other, to let go,
spun toward empty
   by your own thread.

Dust. Dirt, mostly. I walk outside and it stings me,
seeps everywhere, coats eyelashes, lips, neck,
fingernails, shirt cuffs. Seems like it's always windy
here, as if the wind doesn't get anywhere else, just stays
put in a perpetual state of motion. Maybe it circles up
somewhere a few miles away and swings back down
again. And there's always grit in it. The kind that marks
your wrinkles out, the kind that makes you yearn for
water, then turns it to sand in your mouth. It doesn't
matter how I work it, this soil's quit—one more way it's
smarter than me.

Does it seem right to you, lady, that one is punished a
heap and another ain't punished at all?

—Flannery O'Connor, "A Good Man is Hard to Find"

ATTENUATION

The stop extends like a spur
from the door's heel,
but doesn't provoke.

The sacrificial nub accepts
the brunt of wind-pushed,

anger-shoved opens. Stops
can do nothing against
the slam shut. They absorb

damage—the hand
absorbing the impact

before a lover's head
can bump the wall—
I will take the hurt

so you may open.

I remember the first time she called me a baby. I wasn't one, of course. I was a "big girl," too big to cry about the arm falling off a doll, too big to feel the sadness, the weight of broken things. The lack of sympathy I received when I held the arm up made me cry harder. Why was the world so mean? Weak, she said. Crying marked me as a target for the world to hit and hurt. Each time I fell to sadness and the tears came, I repeated her words: *baby, weak.* I had no self control. No wonder I was alone.

Cordyceps are endoparasitic fungi that invade and replace the tissue of the host. When the host dies, the fungi sprout out of it and release spores that enter other hosts.

The tragedy of life is what dies inside a man while he lives.

—Albert Schweitzer

CORDYCEPS

Not a roof, that pinnacle
outside shunting
the rain, hail, sleet the sky drops,
but the highest point inside—

a ceiling where brooding beams
steeple like fingertips, a mind
imprisoning ascending doubts:
speech, smoke, pleas, heat.

Censorious walls lean in,
their barricade of judgment broken
by windows and doors.
The floor shoulders tables, clothes,

spilled wine, books, people—
while the ceiling missionaries
each dexterous, ambitious spider,
each fluttering, bumping moth, shuttering,

then releasing the odd and the lost.

III

Life's wrapped up around one shot. Get love right or get nothing—as if love's a Stalinist dictator demanding complete loyalty while hints of other interests mean death. You can face exile—choose friendships, life partners—but that's not the "jackpot," that's not the "set for life," that's not the "you'll be receiving installments every year till the end of your days" love. And, really? Love is so inflexible, unadaptable, unimaginative as to be a "zero sum," "all or nothing," "you've got your one shot, if you blow it your screwed (or not)" game? Why don't stories generate awe for something more nuanced than the absolute?

Thermophiles are extremophile bacteria that thrive in high-heat environments such as the hot springs of Yellowstone and thermal vents on the ocean floor. Some scientists hypothesize thermophiles might have been the earliest organisms to appear in the high temperature conditions of Earth 3 billion years ago.

Soon you give up, don't look for her anymore, either in the town or at night or in the daytime. Even so you have managed to live that love in the only way possible for you. Losing it before it happened.

—Marguerite Duras, *The Malady of Death*

Thermophiles

Which shadow country beneath stove or bed swallowed you? What drain, what vent, or hostile vacuum ate my earring back, spare key, the ring my grandmother gave me? To be or not to be lost, adored, longed for, obsessed over by the dark hole hiding you and a searching soul: How can my lost stay lost when I burn for them so intensely? I survive on a diet of missing.

In my rented apartment, after a year's worth of cleaning forays and reorganization sorties, the shag carpet finally yielded a tiny yellow shoe, fit for a miniature doll who must have long since learned to hobble barefoot. Is this shoe still missed, as I yearn for my losses? And what if the owner's forgotten it? Such erasure's incomplete, as the fates re-gift this slipper to me. Have my strays surfaced uselessly in someone else's life, or do they enjoy a renaissance of devoted attention? Who understands the biome of the missing? What selective pressures mark its evolution? What adaptive feats, what fantastic creatures will ensure I never recognize something lost returned to me?

I commanded the lives of hundreds, when to arrive, what to do, how to do it faster. I held their food, their shelter, their families' respect. They had to listen. I stood at the window above the floor, watching them move like ants or bees. I could make them all stop, make them frantic, make them weep. They never looked up to see me standing there. They didn't have to. They knew. Once in a while, to remind the rest of them, I'd pluck one from the floor, never to be seen again. It's what I remember most, here, coughing in the wheelchair, looking over the grounds, which are carefully landscaped to please the eye.

Palatine Hill is the central hill of the Seven Hills of Rome.

If you want to find out what a man is to the bottom, give him power. Any man can stand adversity—only a great man can stand prosperity.

—Horatio Alger, Jr. *Abraham Lincoln the Backwoods Boy, or How a Young Rail-Splitter Became President*

From Palatine Hill

A knee-high, flat-topped rock; a fallen trunk,
unearthed roots branching into delta,
offer seats above dank trails.

Height stretches legs and aids vision.
If more than one fits, so much the better:
fellowship. The stump along cleared fields

perfects a mid-day break, as do benches
in mead halls. A seat back appears
when sheer survival shifts

to hours of labor and hours of rest.
Each comes to want, each has, his own chair.
Even if the table's round, any sitter can choose

to break the circle or keep it whole.
The chairman (not the one who builds
or sells, the one who leads), becomes the chair,

and sees the few small steps, sometimes taken,
sometimes not, to throne. Whatever
I may do with it—dine, gain elevation

to change a bulb, stack pages
for recycling—this balanced plateau
maintains allegiance to that distant

tree or rock, beside a brook, above damp ground.

When I told my friend her marriage was doomed, she stopped talking to me for months. What could I do? I couldn't unsee what I saw. I wanted her to be prepared. Like seeing food caught between another's teeth—you can let them go on talking and laughing with everybody cringing, or you can say something. It's not comfortable to do, and people are horrified to hear it, but you speak, for their sake. You pull the handle. What does it matter that no one else comes through the door?

To reject one paradigm without simultaneously substituting another is to reject science itself.

—Thomas Kuhn, *The Structure of Scientific Revolutions*

REVOLUTION

The strain isn't on the water,
   which pours through easily,
      but on the ribbons of linguine,
         waving quantum strings

in the rolling boil, on the elliptical
   orbits of pale zucchini moons,
      and tumbling asteroids
         of squat potatoes—

astral bodies dancing in a watery
   galaxy they wouldn't dream
      of leaving—holding out
         until the water's

almost gone, letting go like August
   comets thudding solidly in mass
      showers into the strainer that embraces
         them as they lose

escaping liquid, the final drops
   neatly channeled earthward
      through the patterned slots.

I'm tired of seeking, of holding heart doors open
waiting for someone to enter—and shutting the doors
after hoping is far harder than opening them. Friends
say persevere; there's someone out there just for you.
Easy for them to say in their compromising lives of
overt familial decency and covert extramarital deceit. I
choose the shirt that matches my eyes. I lock the front
door. I'll be the loudest person at the party.

The floating cone technique is designed to maximize
extraction in an open pit mine.

If you shut the door to all errors, truth will be shut out.

—Rabindranath Tagore

FLOATING CONES

The lampshade
cinches light,
but not as trees do.
Hour-glassing the mini
sun's glare, pinching
the bulb's crown,
directing the glow
to what our hands hold:
reading, the remote, nothing
as we study heart, head,
and lifelines there—
No surprise so many
choose this hat
when seeking illumination,
a floating cone
scooping lumens
out of shadow.

In my son's handwriting, I see the shape of my late brother's letters. The right side arc of "8"s and "O"s thinning to cobwebs, a scrawl, belaboring spins, and skidding along straight paths. The "S" and "3" made up of two distinct motions—forward C backward C, and backward C, backward C—broken in the middle, rejecting the single smooth flair of never lifting the pencil. Each letter etched, a writing cobbled together, paying homage to the notion that even with words before us, understanding takes work.

The average person creates 1/3 ounce of dead skin each week, which is about the weight of a car key. This dead skin combines with other particles to create household dust.

—Hughes Environmental

Latin≥Semitic≥Phoenician≥Greek≈English

Each year   Earth gains forty
  thousand tons of cosmic dust
    drifting from space in   micrometeorites.
We're buried   in dirt, yes,
    and   also   pollen, skin   cells,
bits   of   insect   limbs,
    disintegrated   letters—
    a   gathering of   death's castoffs,
the   broken - down
  and   discarded, too   heavy
to   float   away, like   smoke
or   mist. Stuck   in   the   solid
  a   village of   the   lost
    minute yet   strong   enough
to   assemble   weekly into   matter
no   matter   how   much   I
  wipe   away.

Have you ever spent an afternoon picking hair from the vaccuum's roller brush? Or, maybe you stand at the sink and floss until your gums bleed, trying to save your teeth? How about picking out of the carpet tiny pieces from an over turned 2,000 plus Lego collection, or stepping on said pieces first thing in the morning and trying not to let your cursing wake the house? You need the right kind of mind to know this is the work of love.   But who has that kind of mind?

The 1949 Armistice Agreements, mediated by Dr. Ralph Bunche, established armistice lines at the end of the 1948 Arab-Israeli War.

To make our way, we must have firm resolve, persistence, tenacity. We must gear ourselves to work hard all the way. We can never let up.

—Ralph Bunche

1949 ARMISTICE AGREEMENTS

Holding a simmer
requires finesse.
The burner's blue crown

outperforms electric coils—
fire more nuanced
than current, more visibly

responsive and elemental—

back off from
the roiled boiling
point to bubbling.

For soup's
flavors to meld,
or the richness

of the sauce
to glace for
the true union

of *hawaij* and onion,
conduct the heat
but don't burn.

I don't know where the words came from. Some movie, or book, or more likely a commercial, though I don't suppose any of those offer scripts for fighting. I don't know how "break" made it by my lips. It's a hard word to say, after all, the "b" and "k" require extra work and coordinating with that "r"—it takes some practice. I don't often go for extra effort. You know that. If I said "up" that's positive, right, the way we dream the world as one long climb to better views? It wasn't me; those weren't my words, this isn't my drama. I swear. And for sure there's no one now to lend me words to call you back.

English is so plastic—if you haven't got a word you need you can make it, but to write French you have to be an artist....

—Joseph Conrad

LEAD ($_{82}$PB)

I never knew you
were there, like another's
words colonizing my mouth.
After years of placid wear,
a sudden jar
from the shoved back
kitchen chair
sent you arcing
to the carpet,
heavy as asteroid debris,
or Pluto's oblong moons
constellated
by wreckage.
My whole life I spoke
your poisonous history
made palatable
in layered shades
of lemon drop, mint
green, café au lait,
artfully covering
the cracks in your story.
With a face roséd
in my favorite tone,
you were biding
time, awaiting release—
earthquake, abrasure,
debridement,
bursting on the scene
as so much
complicated dust
wanting me dead.

I was on my way, traveling light, and might not have noticed the thread that tugged, might have shrugged it off as a minor irritation. I don't know where it came from, thin, fragile, what brought me to a halt: the light from a pane of glass on a door held open, shining on a face, that was not smiling, not doing anything that said "this way" or "welcome" or "I'm about to change your life." One thread sparked a "thank you," another look, and lines on the map rearranging themselves without my knowing.

Researchers have managed to create bits of DNA that can stitch themselves together without a helping hand from other molecules....The creation of this super-capable DNA suggests that rare bits of natural DNA might have evolved the same capability in the past. That could alter our thinking about how life began.

—Philip Ball, "Evolved DNA Stitches Itself Up," *Nature: International Weekly Journal of Science*

In Stitches

Just try to close
       seams
without them.
       Lick
the end, pierce the
       needle's
eye, tack the ragged
       lips
of yawning wounds
       together.
Lose the thread and
       splits
begin. Sew twice back
       seats
of pants, cuffs, collars.
       Stitch
tight stressed love
       affairs,
the "is" helixing
       metaphor.
Turn clothes inside
       out,
embroider a dash of
       footprints
marring newly haunted
       snow
stitched from parents
       who
sealed with a finished
       knot
the seam's kiss.

I never mattered much to you, focused as you were on sons who'd run the business, propagate the family name, and earn bragging rights at gatherings. You trained them well. Off grooming themselves, they can't be bothered by their own families, let alone you. So, I spoon the food into your mouth, turn you over, wash your body, take your hand when you're lucidly impotent with rage. No one notes this. No one cares. No one thinks twice about these final moments of decay, and what remains, what continues, who sustains when power's gone.

When a radioactive isotope decays, the initial isotope is called the parent and an isotope resulting from the breakdown is called the daughter.

The wound is the place where the Light enters you.

—Rumi

Daughter Element

Steel wool, rigid plastic, cored
with soap or sponge,
looped tight for extra
baked-on, burned-on
layered messes more stubborn
in sticking than memories
of childhood shame—
the body breaking down,
letting go, before you reach
a bathroom.
You remove what fire
transformed. Circular
scrubbing, scratching,
confronting every speck,
every tumorous thread,
like a cilice for sin,
radiation for cancer,
you retouch the surface
to redeem the pot, the body,
from soot or metastasis,
salvaging each dirty dish.
With an avid mind's devouring
concentration, scour
every shred of contamination,
inspect all sores
needing the erasures
of debridement.
With chemicals, steel, stone,
maggots, strip coating
by coating, so infection
cannot set in,
so healing can begin.

In the hospital bed, she's nervous, scared, worried about the pain. She won't leave, though. She accepts the gift she's giving. Soon she'll be put under, her body not hers for hours of operation. She'll wake up to parts of her missing, incisions, stitches, the genesis of scars that will remind her someone inhabited her, someone took from her what she said she would give, someone left sutures behind before she awoke and reclaimed herself.

In terrane accretion, the rocks from one tectonic plate are accreted to another. Due to plates shifting over time the accreted material can have a distant origin.

Bone marrow transplants can be allogeneic—the stem cells are genetically different but come from someone whose genes partly match those of the recipient.

A coward is incapable of exhibiting love; it is the prerogative of the brave.

—Mahatma Gandhi

TERRANE ACCRETION

To serve, be empty, open,
and steady. Learn to carry

all burdens, those chosen
and acquired—one marrow

allogeneically married
to another. Fulfill your role

when the knife clatters, the fork
scrapes, and bread sops

you clear. Welcome
immersion, the hottest water,

scrubbing, a cleansing rinse,
resting in the palms

of the drainer, before
shouldering the stone again.

Day after day, loaded on trays, sliding down metal rollers, dishes piled with barely nibbled food, glasses full—why fill five or six and drink none? Why do napkins seem the perfect addition to the liquid at the bottom of the glass? Is there some fun in stuffing them down the glass's throat? She shakes, scrapes, or pulls the sopping messes with her fingers and loads the glasses in their sanitizing tray. Every day she accepts what others waste, what others leave behind, what fills and fills the yawning trash bin, the large slick bag replaced as soon as it's filled.

Cerium, a rare earth metal, is used in making carbon arc lights and flints for lighters. Cerium oxide is also used for polishing glass.

Astronomers spent ten years collecting images from the Hubble telescope to create an eXtreme Deep Field image of a sky that is 13.2 billion light years away.

We are "rock people" and not "glass people." Therefore, we do not know anything about glass other than what is on this page.

—ColorWright

Cerium ($_{58}$Ce)

Feeding sweet's
tooth is easy enough,
but crave as well
the coarse trade
of unions:

the abrasion on lenses
sharpening the deep
field image of universe
birth, of stars midwived
into galaxies,

the silt, gravel, rock
terminally morained
into lakes and broken
bluffs of infidelity,

glass people
learning not
to throw stones,

the sandstone kinship
between pear
and potato
found not in groves
or surface tones,
but under the skin,
in firm, grainy flesh
tongued with relish.

She fought the fight against indifference, poured life into her art, writing every day, traveling, studying, reading, editing, always with her mind on what she made, always with her heart open to what she needed to convey. She left it all in good hands. She trusted her work to do the work it needed to get done.

"Too fast for the truth," is a phrase from an 1858 New York Times article on the telegraph which was discussed in a July 28, 2014 article written by Adrienne Lafrance and published in the *The Atlantic*.

Obituaries: "Marya Zaturenska, Lyric Poet Received Pulitzer in '38"

—*New York Times*

Too Fast for the Truth

A few antennae perch on roofs,
silver-pointed stars
catching signals,
embracing snowy static
in expansive metal arms.

Functionally extinct,
relics in these days
of streaming
and satellite dishes,
industrial skeletons
rattling a lesson

in our progressive,
sleek look, ride-
the-newest-wave-
upgrades age:

You might make
the picture clear.
That doesn't mean you'll last.

The line of cars demands the right of way, though not all traffic comes to a stop as it creeps slowly forward, a hearse-headed, multi-sectioned snake, composed of rusting, hubcap-free cars and one battered pick-up truck. No one feels tempted to extend the line. No one cuts it off. This is all they'll ever know of an entire life—a screaming into birth, one special soccer ball covered in red stars, an early marriage, and children, some of whom are not in the line, that winds its way now, through the spiked iron gates.

After the electric light goes into general use, none but the extravagant will burn tallow candles.

—Thomas Edison

THE ELECTRIC LAMP: PATENT NUMBER 223,898

Softer than the softest
bulb, more forgiving
of wrinkles, generous
with shadow—candlelight
sculpts its own world
of sandalwood, lilac, spice—
not like incandescents identified
by wattage, working fine
till they "pop," dropping
in the traces, quick
as a stroke or heart attack
among the overworked.
Only at the end do we reconnect
the bulb's death to fire, "burned out"
we say of those lost lumens—
but with the candle,
wax melts, height diminishes,
one ocher eye gutters
in surprise at too much gust
from the window's slam shut—
tragedy on display. Witness
the luxury of learning light's demands.
A bulb's designed to hide
the cost of burning,
no soliloquies about tomorrows,
while the candle marks its passing
with gray ribbon smoke, sad music rising,
the last note resonating after the keys
are stilled, released at last,
by the curled, black claw
of wick, and the wax, losing heat,
gels back toward solid.

Can I relinquish, allow the day to take its course without my directing its flow? What mark will I leave if I evaporate into letting go? Once, I thought there was some great end toward which I was working, some body of knowledge I was meant to fill. Now it seems it might be better to rest here, to just accept my end of influence, my disappearance. I wouldn't be the first to learn how wandering alone into the desert seeking enlightenment can end.

The Amu Darya, one of the longest rivers in Central Asia, was diverted for agricultural purposes. Eventually it receded from the Aral Sea it once fed and was dammed up 70 miles away. Once one of the world's largest inland seas, the Aral shrank to one-tenth its former size.

Thousands have lived without love, not one without water.

—W. H. Auden, "First Things First"

Amu Darya

We lie down
in beds, and, like
the Colorado, the Indus,
and other dammed
rivers that roar
toward threads
seamed below
desert soil,
we often meet
our end in them, too.

Rushing toward confluence,
fighting the seep of reason
through sands of fatigue,
we sink
toward REM,

open parlor doors
on oceans,
claw the smooth roofs
of pendulumm-ing skyscrapers,
remember how to fly.

Each night we shower,
brush teeth, gargle,
and dream. In our beds
we relearn what being
mostly water means.

If life ignites between us, the weekend getaway hotspots and elaborate five-star dinners won't be the spark. Lay out the simple fare of a cutting board served at a table constellated by condensation from glasses and scuffs of cutlery that slid off dishes being cleared by people who've gathered here for years. Begin with the same tang in your tears as in mine. Don't spice me with anything other than salt.

Biopoiesis is the development of life from non-living matter.

You can find the entire cosmos lurking in its least remarkable objects.

—Wisława Szymborska

BIOPOIESIS

The salt box I bought
in Lithuania is not

the usual cellar haunted
by rice and a twist cap scraping
glass when refilled. Open the hinged lid
and pinch to taste

tides and seaweed. Savor
storm spume, rip currents,
and breezes that blow forever

shoreward. Briny, flaked grit,
dead as ash, alive on food—
Kin to the tang of my blood,
this box of sea dust cells earth
memory and spells me home.

Notes

Steven Heine observes in *Zen Skin Zen Marrow,* "the style of writing of Zen texts has been influenced by 'a variety of east Asian literary games': 1) The extensive use of allusions, which create a feeling of disconnection with the main theme; 2) Indirect references, such as titling a poem with one topic and composing a verse that seems on the surface to be totally unrelated; 3) Inventive wordplay based on the fact that kanji (Chinese characters) are homophonic and convey multiple, often complementary or contradictory meanings; 4) Linking the verses in a sustained string based on hidden points of connection or continuity, such as seasonal imagery or references to myths and legends." I have drawn on many of these elements in crafting these koans.

P. 9: *The Book of Serenity,* Tr. Thomas Cleary, Shambhala Publications, 2005.

P. 25: James Kynge, "Emerging Markets: Fear of Contagion," *Financial Times,* January 30, 2014. https://www.ft.com/content/b201ae8e-89a5-11e3-8829-00144feab7de

P. 35: "Conference between Governor Burnet and the Indians": http://treatiesportal.unl.edu/earlytreaties/treaty.00001.html

P. 45: http://www.anglo-saxons.net/hwaet/?do=get&type=text&id=wdr

P. 66: Sarada Taing, "Clearing Cambodia of Landmines by 2015 was 'Unrealistic,' *Radio Free Asia*, February 27, 2015.
https://www.rfa.org/english/news/cambodia/mines-02272015125810.html

P. 94: Hughes Environmental 15 Facts about Dust:
https://hughesenv.com/15-facts-about-dust/

P. 100: Philip Ball, "Evolved DNA Stitches Itself Up," *Nature International Weekly Journal of Science*, March 31, 2004.
https://www.nature.com/news/2004/040331/full/news04 0329-7.html

P. 106: "Hubble Goes to the eXtreme to Assemble Farthest Ever View of the Universe," 9.25.12,
https://www.nasa.gov/mission_pages/hubble/science/x df.html

P. 106: ColorWright
http://www.rocksandgems.info/faceting_how_to/polishi ng_glass.shtml

P. 108: Adrienne La France, "In 1858 People Said the Telegraph Was 'Too Fast for the Truth,' *The Atlantic*, July 28, 2014.

P. 112: For more on the Amu Darya and other rivers running dry see:
http://environment.nationalgeographic.com/environme nt/photos/rivers-run-dry/#/freshwater-rivers-amu-darya-1_45139_600x450.jpg

RODS AND KOANS is set in Avenir, a twentieth century font designed by Adrian Frutiger.